Welcome to a world of beauty

Arkansas

a world of beauty/Arkansas

Photography by

Hubert Smith

Editors

Ralph W. Sanders
Deborah Wilson
Harry Herget
Patrick McKelvey

FIRST EDITION

Concept-three, Inc., Publishing
Little Rock, Arkansas

Published by Concept-three, Inc.
300 Spring Building
Little Rock, Arkansas 72201

Printed in the United States of America

acknowledgement

The completion of "A World of Beauty—Arkansas" has been a dream I've pursued for years. The opportunity to share this world of beauty with others has made this dream worthwhile. For those who made this opportunity a reality, I owe a lifetime of thanks. I could never list them all, but six deserve special recognition: Robert Sarver—his friendship and generous support will never be forgotten. Alfred Herget, Gerald Brown, Larry Brewer, Buford Dover and John McKenzie—their unbounding faith and enthusiasm has stayed with me from the beginning. To them all a warm and sincere thanks.

Hubert Smith

Library of Congress Catalogue Card Number: 72-93659

introduction

Like the Sculptor's Masterpiece, the varied features of the land
stand out in sharp relief seeming to deny both Time and Man.
Low, rugged mountains subdued by a mantle of hardwood
forests mark the contour of the state from Missouri to the
north and east to Oklahoma on the west. Low hills, masked by
pines, roll across the central and southern regions leveling out
into the grassy prairie to the east, spreading north and south
along the Mississippi River.
Small, rapid flowing streams drop out of the mountains and
large, meandering rivers carve valleys through the forests.
Thousands of lakes mirror the landscape.
It was from this world of beauty that the Nineteenth Century
settlers carved Arkansas.
Plantations developed throughout the eastern region giving
way to smaller farms as the topography rose to the west.
The extensive forests made lumbering second only to
agriculture in economic importance to the state.
Small mills were built originally along the rapid flowing streams
to the north, but with the advent of steam engines, mills
sprang up along the shores of lakes and ponds to the south.
It wasn't until the Twentieth Century that industrialization and
urbanization began to make any headway, and not until the
last two decades did industry begin to replace agriculture in
economic importance to the state.
The eastern region is still dominated by large farms, but the
landscape is increasingly interrupted by growing towns and
industrial parks. The timber industry has grown to be an even
bigger business. The small mill is lost to the forests of Arkansas.
More significant perhaps than the economic shifts is the
changing living environment. Lost to history is the style of life
associated with the small farm and the small country town.

The Well Bucket, the Ole Mill and the Hand Plow are lost to the decay of history. In their places are electric pumps, giant paper mills, and monstrous farm machinery.

The late industrial development is proving to be the greatest resource of the state. While small towns grow toward small cities, and industry replaces farm land, the beauty of the land has not been lost. As Arkansas moves into the Seventies, its industrial future is promising, but Arkansans have the fortunate opportunity of industrializing but not at the expense of their environment.

In the following fifty prints, you have an opportunity to examine the past, a past not untypical to Americans from throughout the middle of the country, and you can view the beauty of the land that is Arkansas.

Hubert Smith has perhaps exceeded his ability as a photographer by his sensitivity to change. By combining the delicacy of the artist with the precision of the camera, he has captured the past and present as they separate. As this book goes to press, many of the rustic subjects of Mr. Smith's work have already been dedicated to history, lost to future generations.

He has combined the same talent and technology in developing his portraits of the Arkansas landscape.

You are invited to travel back in time to recall an era lost to modernization.

Reflections

1

From this land

2

Cypress lake

3

Shadows on a past harvest

4

Pioneer dwelling

5

Mom, the ole wood stove, and apple pie

The ole pitcher pump

7

The ole well bucket

Ozark view

Morning fire

Arkansas in Fall

11

Ozark house

12

Stone chimney

13

Beauty of the Ozarks

14

Rustic fence

15

Wintertime

16

Farm days

17

Working days are over

18

Stockpen

Corners made to fit

20

Clear blue water

21

The ole mill

22

The ole John Deere

23

Smokehouse

The Arkansas River. Awakening.

25

Roses in bloom. Forever.

26

Confederate cemetery

27

Gone to the city

Evening reflection

Waiting for harvest

30

Hidden valley

31

The right time. The right spot.

32

Hidden in the vines

33

Color of the countryside

34

Rustic Gallery

35

Quiet spot

36

Not everything is gray

37

Abandoned

38

Left behind

39

Lonely cypress

40

Mountain valley

41

Construction of years past

42

Man and his environment

43

As far as the eye can see

44

Buffalo River

45

Collapse of the past

46

Looking to the future

47

Remember those cold mornings

48

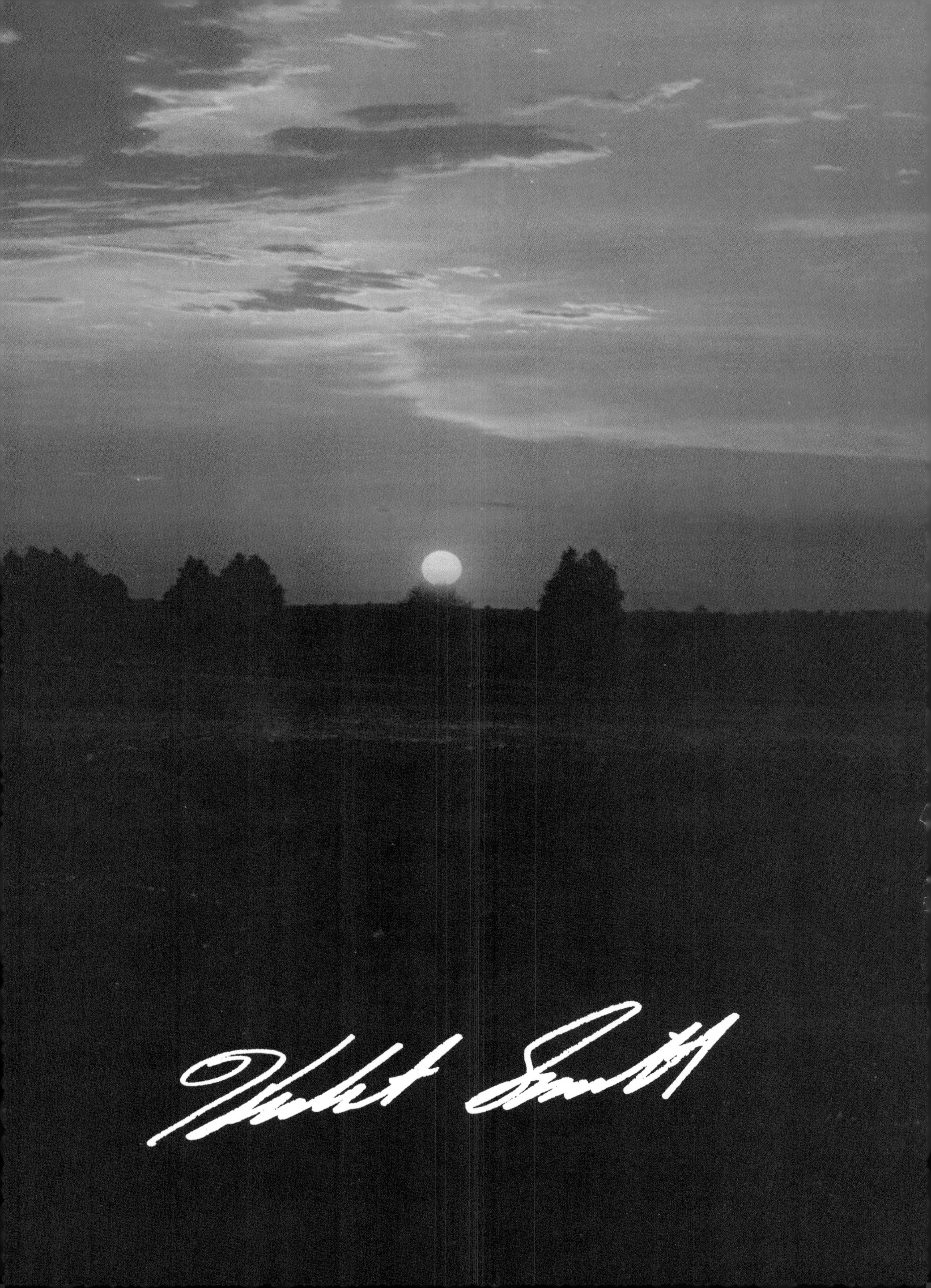

index of locations